VICTORIOUS SECRETS

FOR THE

Breast

CANCER
DIAGNOSEE

Niecy Jones

Victorious Secrets for the Breast Cancer Diagnosee

Copyright © 2021 By Niecy Jones

ISBN: 978-0-578-83974-5

All Scriptures quotations unless otherwise noted is taken from the King James Version of the Bible.

Published by Victorious House Press

DEDICATION

This book is dedicated to my husband and children, who have absolutely always been my biggest cheerleaders. You all are a constant reminder of Gods grace toward me. Whenever I think of you all, I know I have been blessed much more than I could ever deserve. To my family and friends for all of their support, prayers, and well wishes. Thank you for walking with me on this journey. To Dr. Lu., Dr. Dull, and Dr. High, the best Oncologist, Breast Surgeon, and Plastic Surgeon this side of heaven. To Janet Dickmander, NP, and all of the nurses and administrative staff at Rex Cancer Care East Raleigh for their superior care and service. Your uncommon kindness did not go unnoticed. Thank you. To all the women whose example of faith I have been able to follow simply because like Jesus, you were willing to show your scars so that others could believe. To My Lord and Savior Jesus Christ, who told me that Victoria doesn't have all the secrets and that if I would call unto him, he would show me great and mighty things that I knew not of (Jeremiah 33:3 paraphrased). Some Victorious Secrets. I honor him through this book because of the fact that he through his death, burial, and resurrection has made me victorious... period.

CONTENTS

INTRODUCTION

I remember it like it was yesterday. I had felt a lump in my left breast some weeks earlier and watched it for a while to see if it would go away like many of the cystic lumps had done before. However, this lump was different. Finally, after watching it for at least two months, I went to my primary provider to get it checked out. The provider agreed that there was something there that needed to be checked out, so I was immediately referred to get a diagnostic mammogram. The mammogram confirmed that there was a fairly large group of masses growing in my left breast. I was subsequently diagnosed with Stage 2 Her2 positive invasive ductal carcinoma. I remember going to my car, and as soon as I sat in the seat, I began to cry.

I felt like a rush of emotion overtook me due to all the anticipation finally culminating in the moment. Whatever it was, I ugly cried for at least five minutes straight. I called my husband, my family, and some good friends to share the unfortunate news. The next few weeks were a whirlwind as I went to appointment after appointment. I met with several doctors and was started on chemotherapy within the next two weeks. Everything was moving fast, and I felt like I was simply being carried along for the ride. I was there, I was cognizant, but I still couldn't believe I had just been diagnosed with cancer. Me? I had never been sick in my life. I couldn't believe I had to go through chemotherapy and possible radiation. I didn't know how I would get through this, but one thing I did know is that you have to go through to get through. Today, I stand on the other side of breast cancer not as a breast cancer victim but as a breast cancer victor, and I want to share some Victorious Secrets with you.

VICTORIOUS SECRET #1

Gather Yourself

One of my Victorious Secrets for living is getting all the information and not letting emotion carry you somewhere you really didn't need to go. I learned this after seeing people many times get a little information and run with it only to find out later that it wasn't as bad as they thought. My philosophy is that I refuse to expend energy, emotion, or time with unknowns. Early on, I was as cool as a cucumber. I wasn't in denial, but I resolutely gathered all the information by going to my primary physician, getting a more in-depth mammogram, and doing all of the things that needed to be done. Well, when I found out that I had cancer, I believe all the emotions I had harnessed were being let loose at that moment. All the routine questions began to fill my thoughts. *Is this the end for me? Will I die? Why me?* As I sat there in my car, I went through a plethora of emotions.

First I experienced fear, as a Christian, I know we hate to say the word but yes, ever so quickly fear tried to grip me. It was as if my whole life was flashing right before my eyes, and for a brief moment, I felt fear. Then fight took over because I recognized the temptation was presenting itself for me to get into fear. One thing I know is fear may get in your head, but you don't have to let it get in your heart.

I was in fight mode, and I began to immediately wield my sword of the spirit, which, according to Ephesians 6:17, is the Word of God. I had to close the door to fear, and I began to pray and quote scripture. I needed to remind myself of God's promises in that moment and the fact that I have no reason to fear. I also wanted to bring God in remembrance of his Word. "God, you said... I am healed (Isaiah 53:5)." You said, "no weapon formed against me shall prosper (Isaiah 54:17)." I declared God's Word because, as a woman of faith, that is how I learned to fight. I'm still going through all these emotions, so after fight, I got fussy and frustrated as I talked with God. Please know it is okay to get fussy with God. Why pray if you can't be real and authentic? Know that prayer is the one platform where you can say whatever you want and not be judged.

I was talking to God, like, "really?" I was fussing because I lead a very busy life and did not have time in my mind to deal with cancer. I said, "God, I'm pastoring, I'm in school, we were starting an entrepreneurial endeavor, Legacy U Healthcare Consulting and Training Center, a proprietary school I was starting with my daughter. Not to mention I still worked a full-time job, and although I was juggling all of that fairly well, I definitely didn't expect to have to throw a cancer diagnosis in the mix! I was like, "Really, Lord? Are you serious right now?" "You know I ain't got time to fight no cancer." I was just fussing, and I did that for a few moments right there in the parking lot. But then I got back to my fighting in faith. I know I said fight already, but I want to show you the plethora of emotions and the back and forth you may experience, and it's okay.

Wherever your emotions try to take you, know you can't stay there long. I say this because I realize that fear, fussing, and complaining rob you of the energy and posture you need to face and fight the challenges that lie ahead.

That's why I said gather yourself. Gather all your faculties. Wipe away all the tears. You got some decisions to make. I remember gathering myself right there in the parking lot, and I began to think about how what was important in life had not changed. I went over what I knew for certain, and one thing is that God is good. God does not cause sickness and disease. It is a byproduct of the fallen world that we live in. I knew that Satan is the one that comes to kill, steal, and destroy. I also know that Satan is a defeated foe.

Almost as fast as I started to cry, I started making some integral decisions for the journey that lay ahead. Because I am a woman of faith, I immediately knew that this was a faith fight. And I decided right then and there that if I have to fight, I'm glad I know how to.

I said at that moment, "Satan… if you want a fight, you got one" and I made a decision that day that I would make cancer regret that it ever bumbled with this bee."

VICTORIOUS SECRET #2

Family & Friends Matter

People have different ways of handling their family matters. For whatever reason, some people choose not to disclose their diagnosis to their family, while some people tell their family right away. This is certainly a personal decision however; I chose to tell my family right away. Not only did I want them to know, but I needed my circle of family and friends praying for me. I felt a temptation to keep my diagnosis to myself, mainly because I knew that they would be fearful and scared for me, and they were. I knew any attempts to shield them and protect them through nondisclosure might have been met with anger and, in some ways, did not seem fair to me.

Therefore, I decided that being upfront and telling my family was what was best for us. When talking with my children, I let them all have their moment. I will say everyone handles things differently, so be prepared for different responses. All of my children are different, and each one had a different reaction. All of them involved tears in varying degrees, and I let them have their moment. However, I quickly reminded my family and friends that tears were not what I needed, but their prayers, faith, and support. Inevitably, I was so proud to see my children conquer their fear and rise to the occasion to stand with me in this fight day by day.

My friends are like the family that I chose, so I also told some of my close friends that I had breast cancer and solicited their support and prayers. I believe the Word of God when it says, "the prayers of the righteous availeth much" (James 5:16). I don't think I could have navigated this journey as well as I did without the saints' persistent prayers. I also chose to disclose my diagnosis to my church and eventually publicly. I did this for a couple of reasons. One was to deplete the spirit of shame and its power over me. For some reason, the enemy has gotten good at making people ashamed of the things that happen to them even though it is often no fault of their own. I wanted to take that away, and I disclosed it openly and unashamedly.

Another reason I chose to tell people is that I believe that we all have a testimony; any and everything that we go through in life is a part of it. I know the enemy tries to get us to hide our testimony and not share it with others. But I also know that the bible says we overcome by the words of our testimony. I believe as we share our testimony, God can use our challenges to be a blessing to someone else.

Finally, I shared my diagnosis openly because I wanted to be an example of faith.

I knew that this was an opportunity, especially for my children and church members, to see faith at work. It also was a source of accountability for me. I realized that it's easy to say we are in faith when everything is going good, and every day is sunny. But faith is best showcased amid the storms. It is when challenges arise that faith really comes alive. And I literally saw this as my opportunity to sink or swim and I wanted to swim. This was my opportunity to allow my life, like many others in the bible, to be a modern-day tangible example of God's faithfulness. I wanted others to see and prayerfully follow my faith, and then, through that faith and patience, inherit all the promises of God in their own lives. I believe we were created for the glory of God, and it was my turn to give him glory not just with my lips but with my life.

VICTORIOUS SECRET #3

The Importance of Posture

One of the most important things I learned on this journey was the importance of posture. Posture is everything. Your posture is how you stand. When I say posture, I'm talking about how you are going to stand? How are you going to go through this cancer journey? Will you slump over and give in or will you straighten up and stand tall with your chin up and your shoulders squared as you walk through this? I decided that I would stand tall. I pray that you do too.

Your posture has to be a decision that you make on the front end. For me, I had a couple of things that were non-negotiables as I geared up to fight this fight. Firstly, I was going to stay in faith. As a believer, I understood that the bible says the just must live by faith (Hebrews 10:38). I already told you that faith that is not tested might not be real faith. This was my test, and I was hell-bent on passing it. I knew that if I was going to stay in faith, I had to feed myself with the Word of God. I had to encourage myself. For me, that was reminding myself of scriptures. That healing is the children's bread (Mark 7:27). That God is the God that heals us (Exodus 15:26). That, in fact, I am already healed (Isaiah 53:5). I had to remind myself that even though I walked through the valley of the shadow of death, I don't have to fear because the Lord is with me Psalms 23:4). I fed on this because I knew that if this was a faith fight, I had to get my weapons together. The bible says that the weapons of our warfare are not carnal, but they are mighty through God (2 Corinthians 10:4). I had to keep my eye on the Word. This was very important because I remember going into chemo for the first time and sensing a very heavy infirmity spirit as I walked past others.

Your predetermined posture becomes important as you are also tempted to simply fall into the arms of cancer and let it lull you away. I had to constantly remind myself that I had cancer but cancer certainly did not have to have me. I saw the sad, beat down looks on everyone's face. I listened to all the things that the doctors and nurses said I would lose, that was out of my control, and I remember the feeling of despair trying to set in. I told the enemy that day that he may take my hair, he may take some strength, I could definitely stand to lose some of the weight, but he could not steal my joy.

I showed up to my first chemo intentionally wearing my Victorious Period tee as an affirmation of my stance. I was speaking, and talking to all the people, I even ordered pizza for my chemo neighbor and me. I knew that joy was something that I could control. The bible says in his presence is fullness of joy (Psalms 16:11). I knew that if I wanted more joy, I had to stay in his presence. And that's what I did. I did a lot of worshipping, playing songs that magnified God. I magnified him so much until I got small; cancer got small. It wasn't what I was thinking of 24/7. It didn't live rent-free in my head. I had it, but it did not have me. It was then that I realized that not only was I going to be in faith, but I was going to go through this experience in a way that glorified God. I kept saying "God get glory out of this." I believe that we are here for the glory of God. I decided that I wanted Jesus to be seen through my experience. I decided that I wanted to be a sign and a wonder on earth. And that's what I was determined to do.

That's why posture is everything. My faith also allowed me to see the end from the beginning. I had faith for my outcome. I could see the end from the beginning. I recommend that you go on ahead, sis, and see your end from the beginning. Imagine yourself coming out, imagine yourself on the other side of sickness, and then decide today just to walk it out.

One of my mantras was that I knew I would get through this, but I knew that I had to go through to get through. There was no way over it, or under it, and certainly no way around it. It's the same with you. You will get through this. You will be a living testimony. You will overcome! But the first place you have to overcome is in your mind. Set your posture now. You will overcome this. You too are a survivor! You too are victorious! Period!

VICTORIOUS SECRET #4

Mission Minded

As a believer in Jesus Christ, I always believed God for the best outcome. But I also subscribe to the philosophy that our life is all about purpose. And that nothing comes into our lives that God, although he didn't cause it, did allow it to happen. But, because I trust His sovereignty in my life, I had the conviction that this must be about purpose. I immediately began to think about how I could use this to glorify God and help somebody else. I wanted to make the devil mad that he had ever decided to mess with me. I became mission minded because I know that God will turn your problem into your platform.

Creative wheels were already turning in my head, and God gave me an idea for a breast cancer campaign. Because of how I found the lump in my breast only six months after having a normal mammogram, I immediately knew that I had to remind and teach other women the importance of self-breast exams. I began to read and found out that over 40,000 women, especially of color, die every year because of breast cancer. I began to question why, since there is so much treatment for it. I found that many times women were still dying simply because the cancer was not detected earlier. I also realized that had I not been doing monthly self-breast exams, this very well could not have been my testimony. It was then that the "Feeling Myself Movement" was birthed in my spirit.

I called my oldest daughter and told her about my idea to do a PSA educating women on self-breast exams. I told her the concept I had in mind, and she immediately jumped into action. We called a videographer we knew, a few other family members, and the movement came to life. We shared the video on social media, and it was a hit, receiving thousands of views in just a couple of days. I had the opportunity to be on the news because of the popularity of the video. Since then, "Feeling Myself" has become a movement that we celebrate annually during October for Breast cancer Awareness month. Our goal is to reach the same 40,000 that could potentially die from breast cancer every year and who can avoid it through early detection. Being mission-minded also helped me in my own battle. Nothing takes your mind off of your own problems like serving and helping others. You can sit around and sulk, and complain about your situation, or you can make an impact by asking the question, "how can I help others with what I'm going through?"

VICTORIOUS SECRET #5

Keep It Moving

One of my greatest secrets for successfully navigating this cancer journey and what I will tell anybody is to keep it moving. I was so busy that time seemed to fly. At the time, I was pastoring a small fellowship of believers. I was working full time at a very high-stress job. I was in school working on my last two semesters, pursuing a Masters in Nursing Administration when I was diagnosed. Not to mention my daughter and I had just opened a proprietary school for Allied Health programs. I had so many balls in the air that I felt like I couldn't drop simply because I had cancer. So, I kept going.

I would study at chemo, answer emails, make phone calls, etc. Chemo became a planning session for me. When I told one instructor about my diagnosis, they suggested I drop out, but I had come too far to quit. I kept going. One day at a time, one class, one assignment, one doctor's appointment, one thing at a time. I preached every Sunday, and still made most of my obligations. I was amazed at what I was able to do. It was during this time I found out that you will be amazed at what you can do if you just don't quit. During this time, I became intimately acquainted with the meaning of the words in scripture, "Lord give us our daily bread" (Matthew 6:11). My prayer was Lord, if you give me enough days and enough strength, I will get up and do all the things you have called me to do. And because he is faithful, he gave me enough days and enough strength. I was even able to finish school strong with Summa Cum Laude designation at graduation. I was running so much I jokingly tell everyone that I outran cancer.

I am not telling you not to rest, because you absolutely have to when taking chemo, but I am saying cancer does not have to be the end all be all for you. I decided as long as I had breath in my body I was going to keep it moving and I hope you do too. Today as I write, it has been exactly one year since my diagnosis. The year has been jammed pack with ups and downs. I still can't believe all that I went through. I truly believe because I kept it moving, I look back, and it all seems like a blur, what I call my wrinkle in time.

VICTORIOUS SECRET #6

Live Through It

One of the best decisions I made for myself is to live through this cancer journey. I gave myself permission to live. Because in the back of my mind, if this is how I go, I'm going out with a bang. So, I lived. As I told you before, I continued to pursue my goals, worked, and even traveled. Before my diagnosis, I had two trips scheduled out of the country. The first one was a ministry trip that my oncologist did not want me to go on because I had just started my chemo regimen. I complied and canceled the trip. But the second trip was a family vacation that I had been waiting for and anticipating. My sisters and brothers and several sets of cousins were going on a family Christmas cruise, and I was not going to miss it. I talked it over with my oncologist, and of course, he didn't want me to go; however, I made a life decision to go. Of course I took all the necessary precautions by avoiding certain foods, and resting often. I am so glad I went. I didn't have any problems, but I did have the time of my life. I chose to live through it, and I pray that you do the same.

VICTORIOUS SECRET #7

Love Through It

One of my biggest blessings besides my children is that I am married to my biggest champion and best cheerleader. My husband loved me through cancer. He often fussed because many days, he felt that I was doing too much. He took care of me in a way that solidified our marriage and gave me a greater respect for him. I must admit, initially, I wondered how the cancer diagnosis would affect our marriage. Not that he had given me a reason to doubt him, but I had joined a social media cancer group and heard so many horror stories about people's marriages crumbling under the pressures both financially and emotionally. I watched many women going through this journey check out emotionally on their spouses, or vice versa, and I didn't want to give cancer that much power over my life.

I found myself having to intentionally go downstairs and sit with my husband and watch a show on TV the way we always did. I was intentionally eating with him instead of taking all of my meals to my bedroom, which became my favorite place. He saw my struggle, but more importantly, he saw my effort to maintain some sense of normalcy and met me halfway. Many people make the mistake of thinking that the cancer diagnosis only affects them, and while it's true we bear the brunt, don't be fooled into thinking your family is not affected watching you go through it. Blessedly, we walked through this journey together. In fact, it allowed me and my husband to talk on a level we had never spoken on before. Because of the diagnosis, we were forced to have the very necessary conversations about if the unexpected happens? What's next if it does? We talked about our love for each other more openly during this time, and I realize that this experience made us closer and helped us not take each other for granted. We learned that every day with each other is a gift to be cherished.

There were also other issues in the back of my mind when I was diagnosed. How would this affect my marriage relationally? After 24 years, we are still very active. We had a robust sex life. Fortunately, sex had been something that was never broken in our marriage, and I wondered how being sick would affect our relations and our relationship. I talked with my oncologist about it, and I also prayed about our sex life. With all that was going on, I did not want it to deteriorate. And blessedly, it didn't. Call me strange, but I had made a covenant with myself years ago never to turn my husband down sexually. I had been able to keep that vow, but now I wondered how cancer would change that. Would it change it? How would he take it? These are all thoughts that were playing in the back of my mind. The good news is everything worked out fine. You will have to wait for the sister book "Victorious Secrets for Marriage" for all the details.

Suffice it to say, we are here, living, and loving each other more than ever. And I encourage you to continue to love also. Be honest, be patient, and don't shy away from the very real and often difficult conversations. Your partner is on this journey with you so let them be.

VICTORIOUS SECRET #8

No Hair, Don't Care

I wish I could tell you that everything was fine and dandy. I wish I could tell you that I didn't have days where I felt bad or that my self-image wasn't under attack this entire journey. But if I did, it wouldn't be the truth because cancer absolutely has the potential to be devastating to a woman's self-image, if you let it. One of my life philosophies is not giving mental energy to things that are out of your control.

I already knew that my hair was going to fall out with the chemo. I figure I could sit around and cry a river over hair. Or I could own it. I decided to own it. Before my hair came out, I had already looked into having a customized wig made. Of course, it was challenging going from my normal hairdo, which was a short natural cut to a whole wig.

Nonetheless, I wasn't going to let hair steal my joy. I wore that wig faithfully until my hair began to grow back and I could get another style. By getting out in front of it, I was able to retain some sense of control over my self image. Secondly, I knew that a bilateral mastectomy was not my idea of sexy. However, I got it in my mind that the trade-off would be the nice new pair of breast I was getting. And they became my light at the end of the tunnel. I don't know what challenges you will have to face or how it messes with your self-image. But whatever you do, own it. Control what you can, how you can and leave the rest to God. Everything will be fine. Make a decision today to refuse to give your mental energy to things that are out of your control. I owned it and I encourage you to own it too because at the end of the day, it is what it is.

VICTORIOUS SECRET #9

Your Environment Matters

Your environment matters. I hope I don't come off as a superwoman who could leap tall buildings in a single bound. But I will say that I saw what was possible because of the environment that I was in. I saw my Pastor, Bishop Rosie Oneal, navigate cancer in such a glorious way, and my faith was lifted simply by watching her. I had learned that there is no way to lose from her. That even death is a win for the believer. I knew the Word of God, and I believed that our God was bigger and that I too am a sign and a wonder.

I believe that we overcome by the blood of the lamb and the word of our testimony (Revelations 12:11). I believed that God had me and that Christ was carrying me through every step of this dark season. I believe that I can do all things through Christ that strengthens me (Philippians 4:13). I believe all things are possible if you only believe (Mark 9:23). I learned all those lessons in the church. I fully give the credit for my mindset, temperament, and posture during this season to the environment of faith that is central to my life. If I could only share one secret with you – surround yourself with people that encourage you, are praying for you and, help you be the best version of yourself. I encourage you to get in a faith-filled environment where you can know that you too are victorious. Period.

VICTORIOUS SECRET #10

Death Doesn't Sting

I told you to gather yourself. Take hold of your emotions. I also told you that one huge emotion trying to grip me was anxiety over thoughts of death and my demise. I knew all the scriptures and stuff, nonetheless, it tried to get me. Death had never been so close in my mind until I received that diagnosis. I found myself thinking about it all the time. The thought of death was like a ghost, lingering over me most days and even at night in my dreams. I knew that I had to get some perspective on not just life but death.

Like most people, I had always seen death as an enemy—something to be avoided instead of accepted. However, as I read the bible, I was introduced to a death that was not to be afraid of, and in fact, when the time comes, it is more to be embraced than feared.

One of the writers in the bible said something to the effect that death had lost its sting (1 Corinthians 15:55). That scripture reminded me of certain types of bees that lose their ability to sting anyone else once they sting someone. My Christian faith teaches that Jesus Christ let the bee sting him so to speak. He let death sting him so that death now for the believer doesn't sting. Death for us is what my pastor calls a limousine ride to glory. The bible says that to be absent from the body is to be present with the Lord (2 Corinthians 5:8). Once I got the right perspective on death, I realized that I had no reason to fear. Although I want to live to be 100+ and am by no means inviting death, I stopped fearing death. I stopped seeing death as the big black ghost in the room when I realized that death doesn't sting.

In fact, I wrote a poem entitled cancer is a car. It says...

cancer is a car, carcinoma to be exact. Not the big C or anything like that. But it's forever reduced in my mind, and forever stamped in time when God revealed this simple line to me that cancer is only a car. See, cancer is a car, and we all need a ride to the other side.

And like any long ride, I may have fallen asleep on this side, but when I opened my eyes, I realize that cancer was only my car.

So entranced by his glory…

What celebration, what liberation, what a transformation, and what a destination……

With all my history in my rearview, the truth is this is what I've been living and dying to get to.

So, as I watch the Son rise with a gleam in his eyes that can't be described or sermonized…

As I worship with Angels and see family and friends… again..

As I put on my white robe and my crown decked out with gems…

As I walk on white sandy beaches and golden streets and spend Sabbaths without end...

Be encouraged. His promise is true... in Christ, we really do win!

Because if I could only tell the whole story from my place in glory... you too would say surely... cancer was only her car.

I pray that you get this same revelation. Don't let the enemy paralyze you with fear of death. I want to tell you a secret I found out in the word of God. Death does not sting.

In closing I pray that these victorious secrets will help you as you gear up to slay cancer. I hope that you too can disarm cancer of its grip on your life and especially your mind. I hope that you come to know that cancer is not the big C. In fact if you noticed every time I write the word cancer anywhere at anytime, I write it with a little "c". This is because in my life there is only one big "C" and his name is Jesus Christ. And can I tell you one last secret. Christ is bigger than cancer. Therefore, I refuse to give cancer the designation in my life that is only reserved for him. Christ is the Big "C" and It is because of him that I am victorious. And so are you.

In closing I would like to whisper a short prayer for you.

> Father in the name of Jesus, I pray for the person that is reading this book. Father I declare that they are strong enough for this season of their life. I pray for them to be strong and very courageous. I thank you that you are the God that heals us, and they will come to know you personally as a healer. I thank you that you will keep them in perfect peace, and that their minds and thoughts are at rest. I thank you that even though they walk thru this cancer journey that they have no reason to fear because you are with them. I pray that you give them superior providers and all the support that they need. I pray

that they have all the resources that they need and that every need is met with heavens' best. I declare victory for the person reading this book and that they know that they are victorious in Christ. It is in Jesus' name that I pray. Amen.

I pray that the victorious secrets in this book though not exhaustive, help you just as they have helped me. May the Lord bless and keep you throughout this journey and may you emerge on the other side of cancer Victorious. Period!

www.ingramcontent.com/pod-product-compliance
Lightning Source LLC
Chambersburg PA
CBHW061757040426
42447CB00011B/2351